How to Use Translation to Grow Your Business

WINN TRIVETTE II, MA

Copyright © 2018 Winn Trivette II, MA

All rights reserved.

ISBN-13: 978-1720104315

CONTENTS

0 Introduction   Pg 1
1 Your Company's Translation Strategy   Pg 4
2 New Frontiers Vision   Pg 10
3 Internet Research   Pg 13
4 Choose A Translation Partner   Pg 18
5 Last Thoughts   Pg 24
6 7 Next Steps   Pg 26
7 Thank You   Pg 30
8 About the Author   Pg 31

This page left blank intentionally.

INTRODUCTION

What enables the wise sovereign and the good general to strike and conquer and achieve things beyond the reach of ordinary men is foreknowledge.

- Sun Tzu, ancient Chinese philosopher

Welcome to *How to Use Translation to Grow Your Business*!

The interdependent global marketplace makes every business an international player.

Why do some firms in an industry win and achieve success while others fail?

A Fortune 500 company survey once showed 55 percent make use of *competitive information* in composing business strategy.

This business intelligence – Sun Tzu's foreknowledge – can be enhanced through the application of a corporate translation strategy.

Your own company or firm can gather business intelligence *via translation* to reap profits when your rivals do not.

While the world economic chessboard is, for the moment, dominated by English, vital information also appears in Spanish, Portuguese, and French, for example.

Thus, with a translation partner, proper strategy, and vision, any company from Tokyo to Tallahassee can project its goods and/or services to new frontiers beyond its current borders.

And yes – leave the competition behind!

The following argues for collaboration with a translation partner like Professor Winn to implement a novel translation strategy to gain foreknowledge to help your business create new market space even in highly competitive industries.

Stop relegating translation to an afterthought in the operation of your business.

Instead, think of translation as a *pro-active* part of energizing your business strategy.

Unleash the power of translation to gain business intelligence and grow your business to reach these unserved consumers and outwit your rivals at the same time.

Let Internet Research in Spanish, Portuguese, French, or any other language to attract new clients and rescue you from the conventional wisdom of your current industry.

Professor Winn's New Frontiers Vision marries the "blue ocean" (*) approach with translation to tap uncontested market space and drive potentially explosive company growth.

While the "blue ocean" approach is not new, its combination with a comprehensive translation strategy is.

Read on for more details as outlined in each section below.

Section 1: Your Company's Translation Strategy – Learn how a methodical approach to translation benefits your business.

Section 2: New Frontiers Vision – Discover new clients via translation in untapped or underserved markets.

How to Use Translation to Grow Your Business

Section 3: Internet Research – Let your translation partner seek and report valuable market information.

Section 4: Your Translation Partner – Add a reliable translator to your team and find solutions to your translation needs.

Section 5: Last Thoughts – Get final thoughts on the New Frontiers Translation Strategy as a means to grow your company's clients.

Section 6: 7 Next Steps – Follow these steps to initiate your own actionable New Frontiers Translation Strategy.

Section 7: – Thank you.

I look forward to helping you grow your company's profits!

Professor Winn Trivette II, MA

Sign up for email updates about translation and receive the e-report, *7 Ways to Lower Your Translation Costs*: **https://atranslationace.com/01.**

* Professors W. Chan Kim and Renée Mauborgne are the authors of the sensational business theorem as explained in their seminal text, *The Blue Ocean Strategy*, released in 2005.

1: YOUR COMPANY'S TRANSLATION STRATEGY

Without a translation strategy, your company could be vulnerable in the interdependent global marketplace of the 21st century.

More than a language strategy, a translation strategy drives the internationalization of a company's strategic planning so its products and/or services can compete in the international market while sustaining its ability to monitor and maintain the expansion.

Why Your Company Needs A Translation Strategy

The following is a think piece for companies to re-evaluate their strategic goals by implementing simple measures to gain a competitive advantage in the world business arena.

Definition of a Translation Strategy

Does your company already have a language strategy? Good start!

A step further is using the power of translation to not just speak a new language, but to exploit a language to create a differential advantage with competitors.

Make your firm's products or services distinct from rivals by creating and maintaining a superior more than just a competitive offering.

A proactive approach to gaining sustainable market share is possible through the coin of the realm in the international economy – information.

Of course, not all of the valuable information in global business is in English.

When you operate in a Spanish or Portuguese-speaking market, for example, your company needs business intelligence gleaned from information sources in these areas.

While researching, designing, delivering, and marketing your product or service, your translation strategy can operate alongside.

A systematic program (outlined below) can gather and convert data to fuel the business intelligence (BI) your company needs.

Internet research in Spanish, Portuguese, and French, for example, can be conducted and translated into English.

Your translator is a business partner, a part of your team, to increase satisfaction and positively impact the bottom line.

Do a Translation Needs Analysis

A blueprint for a comprehensive translation strategy begins with a consultation with a certified translator like Professor Winn.

An initial discussion should center upon conducting a comprehensive **translation needs analysis**.

Eleven components would include at a minimum:

1. What are the company's goals in the next few years?

2. Is management on board with implementing a company-wide translation strategy?

3. Is the company website in the target market language?

4. What markets does the company currently operate or plan to operate?

5. What are the languages spoken in these markets?

6. What type of information and possible sources in Spanish or Portuguese, for example, should be consulted?

7. How often will information be consulted and subsequently translated?

8. What other types of documents will you likely need translate?

9. What is the expected deadline for these translated documents?

10. Who or which department will be responsible for managing the translations in the company?

11. What is the expected budget to fund translations throughout the year?

Above all, remember the Pareto Principle – the so-called 80/20.

That is to say 20 percent of your activities will account for 80 percent of your results.

Thus, let your own company quickly and effectively draw up a road map for using translation to gain an "unfair" competitive advantage over your peer rivals.

4 Benefits of a Translation Strategy

A company's investment in a translation strategy yields four main results.

First, gain a competitive edge.

Yes, business literature is replete with trite with articles about "competitive advantages."

However, with methodical preparation for managing translations, your company would be a step ahead of the competition.

If you receive information in a report or other document in Spanish, Portuguese, or French, for example, you will already have a process in place.

Time is saved and fast information ahead of rivals helps your business to nimbly outwit peers in a market.

Any edge – especially linguistic when operating in international markets – is a definite advantage.

If your company submits bids for contracts, letter-perfect English translations from original Spanish, Portuguese, or French texts could make the difference in the competition for business.

Second, learn more about your market (customer).

Internet marketing research in Spanish or Portuguese can help a company select the right media, such as TV, radio, newspaper or print to reach customers.

Product or service-driven companies may struggle to keep pace with changing or evolving marketplaces.

A corporate translation strategy allows collection of business intelligence in the language of international markets.

Third, discover new products or services for your company.

An enterprise that enters a new market can especially take

advantage of translations to create products or services to meet customers' needs.

Expansion of a product line or offer of services could result from more consumer information from business intelligence gained through translation.

Internet market research not only yields publicly-available information about competitors and customers alike.

A report about a new trend in an international market is likely to appear in a local newspaper or magazine.

An effective translation strategy allows a rapid response to ensure the customer has the product or service desired in a shorter production and delivery time to market.

Lastly, a company can save on translation costs.

Even the smallest enterprise in the global economy, from time to time, needs translation.

Instead of ad hoc projects, a comprehensive language and translation blueprint for your business yields greater consistency and uniformity.

Thus, a company can control costs better with good planning and a retainer fee for translation.

Your translator is always available to help you expand the reach of your products and/or services and acquire more customers which is good for the bottom line.

Conclusion

Your translator is your business partner.

Thus, translation is not an extra cost, but an investment in the growth of company profits.

How to Use Translation to Grow Your Business

A comprehensive way to manage the need and use of translations can actually save the firm money in the long-run.

So, start to define your translation strategy today and gain a competitive advantage in the world business arena.

Find "untapped buyers" when you embrace the New Frontiers Strategy discussed in the next chapter.

Contact Professor Winn for a free quote for your translation project: winn@atranslationace.com

2: NEW FRONTIERS VISION

From Internet firms to circuses, more companies seek a "blue ocean strategy" to make their competition irrelevant.

Could your company benefit from frictionless market sectors and opportunities?

Let your certified translator like Professor Winn help!

New Frontiers Vision

Ever since 2005 when Professors W. Chan Kim and Renée Mauborgne originally explained this sensational business theorem in their seminal text, *The Blue Ocean Strategy*, the business world was hooked.

In the text, the two authors provide an analysis of 150 strategies from 30 industries spanning the last 100 years.

The good professors advise abandoning the current cut-throat "red ocean" thinking and operation in your industry and instead seek new opportunities, the so-called "blue oceans."

A well-crafted corporate translation strategy can help companies, law firms, real estate offices, and even hotels open blue ocean markets.

New consumers occupy these unchartered market spaces where your products and services can create demand.

These so-called "Third Tier unexplored" non-consumers are your future customers per the follow-up text by the good professors, *Blue Ocean Shift*.

How to Use Translation to Grow Your Business

Add translation and Internet Research.

The result is the New Frontiers Vision for your company.

The New Frontiers Vision is a "blue ocean" approach mixed with a translation strategy to attain *actionable business intelligence* to both grow your client base and thus profits.

For example, a US-based company operating in Latin America could employ a Spanish and Portuguese to English translator to discover new underserved market spaces that are unknown even to your rivals.

Do you have the courage to locate and embrace these untapped buyers?

Implement Your New Frontiers Vision Through Translation

How can a translator help your company implement *your* New Frontiers Vision?

Discovering untapped consumers in an international market sector requires information.

The best financial and marketing data about your target market is probably in the local language!

Thus, use Internet Research in Spanish, Portuguese, or French is essential for three reasons. (Read more in the next section).

Let translation grow your business through the New Frontiers Vision.

Conclusion

Start your New Frontiers Vision today.

Winn Trivette II, MA

Use translation as a secret powerful advantage to win the race with rivals to create a new market space.

Find a new market segment to supply your product and/or services.

Leave behind the "red ocean" cutthroat competition and vapid conventional wisdom of your current industry.

Dare to compile Sun Tzu's foreknowledge through Internet Research (see the next section).

Differentiate your product/service mix to outwit your rivals.

Read Section 6 – 7 *Next Steps* - for more details on the implementation of your New Frontiers project.

3: INTERNET RESEARCH

Internet Research is the main driver of the New Frontiers Vision.

It is a cost-effective means to gather business intelligence to not only learn a rival's plans, but how to best position your company in a new untapped market.

New clients are waiting for your goods and/or services. Find them!

The following is a detailed discussion of how Internet Research (primarily in Spanish, Portuguese, and French) can yield actionable information to guide your firm to greater profits.

While the author emphasizes the benefits of translating Spanish, Portuguese, and French market research (his strengths!), the New Frontiers Vision is just as applicable in other languages as well.

Preparing an Internet Research Report

Collecting business intelligence is totally an ethical, simple and valuable technique to enhance your market research.

Involve your translator partner to enhance market data with more details drawn from the non-English sources!

Use research from the Spanish, Portuguese, and French Web for in order to create an uncontested market space – a New Frontier.

Winn Trivette II, MA

Competitive Business Intelligence consists of three major units:

Strategic intelligence analyzes a competitor a competitor's future goals, current strategy, assumptions held about itself and the industry, and capabilities.

Tactical intelligence centers on a competitors' terms of sale, their price policies and the plans they have for changing the way in which they differentiate one or more of their products from yours.

Counter intelligence helps to defend your company secrets so you are better able to shield your plans as you in turn lean more about your rival's intentions in the market.

From customer surveys, presentations at industry conferences, and other public information, your translator can help your team position the company precisely in an underserved market.

For example, your translator could monitor news from a group of Latin American oil companies who gather for a conference in Sao Paulo.

Then, a certified translator like Professor Winn would be necessary to ferret out nuggets of data in both Spanish and Portuguese.

Or, in another case, your office could receive live dispatches from your translator who attends the said conference.

Actually, a fact-finding mission to trade show is a common "hands on" technique to size up a rival's plan.

Above all, Internet Research outside of English is indispensable to open virgin market spaces for your goods and/or services in the global interdependent economy.

5 Reasons to Invest in Internet Research

First, your company is able to quickly gather information about a distant market and analyze the suitability of your product/services mix.

Second, research by your Spanish and Portuguese financial translator of publicly available reports, market surveys, or press clippings helps your company understand the hidden pain points that limit the current size of the industry and discover an ocean of untapped customers.

Third, your company learns (more) about the current competition and how your company can modify products, services, and/or message in the market – thus creating a new frontier for your goods and/or services.

Fourth, your company avoids surprises – namely what *Harvard Business Review* termed – "Disruptive Innovation."

Your rivals want to thwart your success in the market.

Will a surprise technology, product, or process creep up and challenge your market dominance?

Internet Research driven by translation gives you Sun Tzu's foreknowledge!

Finally, you receive a crisply-written report in English with business intelligence to facilitate entry into a new unchartered market safe from rivals or simply introduce a new product or service.

Harness the power of translation to carve out your new market niche and turn current non-customers into big buyers of your products and services.

Analysis of Internet Research

Winn Trivette II, MA

Professor Winn can write your Internet Research Report in perfect English.

The length of your Internet Research report depends on the nature of the topic, and the number of sources.

If you are a business who plans to enter an underserved market, expand your research to include the Spanish, Portuguese, and French webs.

As an article in *Quartz* states, "While English may be emerging as a bridge language, a wave of media is being produced in other languages, in newspapers, on television, and on the Internet."

Spanish, Portuguese, and French are the third, fifth, and ninth languages of the Internet, respectively.

Once you have your report, unite your sales and marketing teams to examine the Internet Research Report.

What are the best practices?

One area to examine is any misunderstandings concerning your product or service.

Use the following information to avoid competition with your rival and thus open a new market space:

***Competitors' Universal Selling Point in relation to your products/services

***Features to add, change, or eliminate

***Marketing message to attract interest and create demand

***Problems with any sales tactics to get new customers.

A meta-approach to valuable Internet Research – searching information in three languages! – plus English guarantees a comprehensive review of market conditions.

Conclusion

At heart, gathering business intelligence is focused on enhancing decision making based on the foreknowledge gained.

Success in business often rests on a series of good decisions.

Internet Research by a certified, veteran translator like Professor Winn provides you good information to reach good decisions.

The Spanish, Portuguese, and French webs become available to mine for strategic information instantly with assistance of a translator partner.

Competitive global firms have a growing need for the necessary information on which to base decisions, especially in search for New Frontiers – uncontested market space and new consumers for your goods and/or services.

What are your areas of research?

4: CHOOSE A TRANSLATION PARTNER

Small, medium, and large companies will experience a language barrier when expanding into countries that do not share its home country language.

The importance of language differences in international companies cannot be dismissed or ducked.

And no, your bilingual employees, however well-meaning, nor online translator websites, are competent to handle the translation load.

The following examines how to choose a translation partner and its four advantages.

Choose a Translation Partner for Your New Frontiers Strategy

The level of Business Intelligence gained through translation will influence the direction of your small, medium, and large company.

In order to find and engage new clients in an underserved market, a translator needs to bring a certain amount of skills.

First, he or she should be a certified translator.

In the United States, translators are certified in two main ways: 1) a university program or 2) a certification from the American Translators Association (ATA).

Professor Winn, who graduated from the Translation Studies program at Florida International University (Miami, Florida), is certified to render Spanish, Portuguese, and French documents into English.

He is also a professional member of the Association of Translators & Interpreters of Florida.

Second, your translator should be a native speaker of English – if translating into English.

Translators must convert documents into their own native language.

In the case of Professor Winn, given his native language is English, he should only render documents into that language.

Third, he or she should have superb English writing skills.

The most important language in translation – is your mother tongue!

In the end, one has to write a document in spotless English (in the case of Professor Winn).

Sharp writing skills – including good grammar and precise punctuation – are indispensable for a translator to convert your documents successfully.

Fourth, your translator should have a minimum five years of experience.

Make sure your translator has the expertise and experience to successfully bring your project to a close!

Fifth, he or she should have cultural competence in the original language.

Language is culture.

Your translator must be able to convert meaning in the original language (like Spanish, Portuguese, or French for

Professor Winn) into English.

Given Professor Winn's many years living and teaching English in South America and study of Spanish, Portuguese, and French, he is culturally expert at understanding these languages and changing them into English.

Sixth, your translator can conduct extensive Internet, database, and media research into companies and individuals to provide clients with an accurate assessment of the status, legitimacy, general background, and overall reputation of a subject company and its principals.

Finally, he or she should have knowledge in the area of your business.

Subject expertise is also another competence a translator brings to the table.

Vocabulary and expertise derived from book smarts or work experience are signs of a translator ready for the task.

Now read how companies gain five distinct advantages **partnering with a translator**.

5 Advantages to Partner with a Translator

In order better to deal with foreign markets, these firms should partner with a translator or risk a loss of business.

Business or legal documents in Spanish, French, or Portuguese need translation sometimes in a pinch.

Today's businesses gain five (5) key advantages by forming a partnership with a freelance translator like Professor Winn:

1. Access

Your business pact with a freelance translator ensures direct access.

When you receive a translation project at an odd hour, chances are your translation business partner can help.

That's a distinct advantage over big box translation firms.

Your freelance Spanish, Portuguese, or French to English translator can discuss your project and provide you peace of mind – your project will receive due diligence on a schedule convenient to you.

When you need precise, prompt, and professional translations, contact Professor Winn!

2. Gain a Competitive Advantage

Time is money.

Perhaps you need a legal document or land survey translated from Spanish to English before an important meeting the next day. But, the meeting is unexpected.

Small and medium companies can least afford this vulnerability which could sink or save an important deal. And which deal is not significant to the bottom line?

Because of your pact with a freelance translator, the flexibility from direct access to a partner who cares about your business, you've gained a competitive advantage.

Now that meeting can go on as planned.

Rapid turnaround is another advantage of working directly with a professional freelance translator who knows your business and you know he or she is in your corner rooting for your success.

Let Professor Winn help with a comprehensive strategy for managing your translation.

Partner with Professor Winn for your Spanish, Portuguese, and French to English translations today.

Send details of your translation project for a free quote: winn@atranslationace.com.

3. Better and Stronger International Presence

While English is the *lingua franca* of international business, your small or medium-sized company knows how valuable the language of your target market is.

Your business pact with a freelance translator grants you a full license to explore new products or acquisitions in your target market. You know your translation partner is available to help grow your success.

Small, medium or large-sized companies all experience growing pains abroad.

Stop!

Don't think of language barriers if your target market speaks Spanish, Portuguese, or French!

Grow your global footprint confident in the fact that Professor Winn supports your initiatives.

Gain a better understand your target market today via the New Frontiers Vision!

4. Minimize Miscommunications

Avoid any miscommunications with documents from your target market!

How to Use Translation to Grow Your Business

Don't deal in Spanish, Portuguese, or French-only papers.

Get a trusted translation from your partner!

Trust but verify the word of a business partner in your target country.

Your own independent translation can corroborate any document from the target market and give you an added layer of protection against any (potentially costly) misunderstanding.

5. Exploit Impeccable Internet Research Skills

The global connect Knowledge Economy tracks seamlessly with the explosion of information on the Internet.

However, the key is the knowledge of where to find answers to your questions.

Today, expansion abroad requires combining language competence, translation acumen, and research power.

Professor Winn – a veteran translator – is capable of researching the Spanish, Portuguese, and French webs to find the answers to your questions about the New Frontiers market areas.

Conclusion
Now you can successfully partner with a translator to help you implement your New Frontiers Strategy.

Get your Spanish, Portuguese, or French-language documents into English to avoid any miscommunication due to language barriers.

Contact Professor Winn: winn@atranslationace.com

5: LAST THOUGHTS

Companies that truly want to succeed have the onus for the collection of business intelligence in the modern Knowledge Economy.

Sun Tzu's *foreknowledge* – an "unfair" advantage for your firm is available. Seize it!

Yes, you can combine the power of translation and Internet research to expand the reach of your products and/or services to new consumers.

Create a **New Frontiers Vision** to define your new mission, analyze your situation, conduct research, identify your target market, and develop your marketing mix.

Write down the idea for a new mission to open untapped markets and now outline it. Flesh out its main concepts.

The subtopics are not as important as the broad strokes at this point.

Are you ready for your firm to work with an experienced certified translator who can also conduct vital Internet Research?

It is cliché, but knowledge is power.

However, knowledge about underserved consumers for your goods and/or services provides you distinct edge to outwit your rivals.

You have to decide to pursue this business intelligence and

How to Use Translation to Grow Your Business

analyze and harness it to advance the bottom line of your company.

Now, you have the New Frontiers Vision to do just that.

Read on for an outline of seven (7) immediate steps to take now!

6: 7 NEXT STEPS

The best big idea is only going to be as good as its implementation.

- Jay Samit, a digital media innovator and pioneer

The following are seven (7) steps to implement your New Frontiers Vision.

1. Analyze the current status of your company.

Where do you operate?

Where would you like to enter a market?

Where are possible prospects? Do likely threats lurk?

Is your product mix adequate for a New Frontiers market?

Beyond a SWOT analysis, seek a more 360-degree view of your company in the market encompassing past, current and future perspectives.

2. Ask and Answer: What unique abilities or assets does the business provide to new consumers? Does the Unique Selling Point (USP) need an update?

What long-term value can be given to these new customers while maintaining a competitive advantage?

Will you simply introduce existing products to the new consumers?

Or will new products and new USPs be necessary?

3. Embrace the New Frontiers Vision fully. Use translation as a tool to access current noncustomers in new market spaces.

Resolve to create a "blue ocean" market space to outwit the rivals.

Recognize the power of translation to introduce existing or new products and/or services to these nonconsumers.

4. Name the New Frontiers Designated Market (FSDM) – the space of untapped consumers where you will introduce your goods and/or services.

What type of business intelligence is needed?

What are possible sources for analysis of the new market space?

What languages are involved?

Which languages should be involved?

Given the Digital Knowledge Economy today, Internet Research is essential for gaining information about new markets.

Entry into the underserved Latin America market requires knowledge of Spanish and Portuguese.

The latter is indispensable for understanding Brazil and the former for the other countries.

5. Consult a certified experienced translator (Spanish, Portuguese to English for Latin America, for example) as a team member.

Consult the translator to build cultural awareness among staff.

Be sure prospective candidates also possess strong research skills – in English and the other languages (Spanish, Portuguese, staying with the Latin American example).

The Marketing and Sales Departments should accept the new translator as a partner to deliver results in the New Frontiers Designated Market (NFDM).

Each area can rely on the translator for language solutions anytime during entry into the new untapped market.

6. Give the translation partner the first assignments.

Unleash the combined power of translation and Internet research!

Make the tasks in the form of questions.

For example, three (3) questions about entry into the Colombia technology area.

***What is the size of the market opportunity that this project might open up?

***How will the project explore the market potential?

***What are the risks (technical, commercial and environmental) to project success?

7. Conduct Post-analysis.

Critically review the translator's initial report. Are the answers accurate?

How to Use Translation to Grow Your Business

Does the preliminary investigation warrant more research?

How can a translator continue to assist implementation of your New Frontiers Vision project?

THANK YOU

Congratulations!

You are now prepared to move your company from the "red ocean" cutthroat competition and vapid conventional wisdom of your industry to a "blue ocean" New Frontiers Vision.

Serve these nonclients with your goods and/or services and leave the competition in the dust.

Boost profits. Grow your international footprint.

Partner with a certified translator like Professor Winn for Spanish, Portuguese, and French to English translations to create your own New Frontiers Vision today: **winn@atranslationace.com**

A Small Favor

If you enjoyed this book, please consider leaving a review in the book store you purchased it from. Reviews are helpful for feedback so authors may improve their product.

Thank you!

ABOUT THE AUTHOR

Winn Trivette II, is a certified veteran translator of business and legal documents from Spanish, and Portuguese, to English.

He also is a professional member of the Association of Translators & Interpreters of Florida.

For more than 10 years, he has helped clients communicate their message to the world in English. He also teaches English as a Second Language and authors educational books for international students.

Let Professor Winn contribute to your business success today: **winn@atranslationace.com.**

www.ingramcontent.com/pod-product-compliance
Lightning Source LLC
Chambersburg PA
CBHW030044230526
45472CB00005B/1667